My Christmas Prayer Book

Luke 2:1–20 for children

Written by Sarah Fletcher

Illustrated by Bob Watkins

CONCORDIA PUBLISHING HOUSE · SAINT LOUIS

The donkey did not mind his load
As Joseph walked and Mary rode
Along the road to Bethlehem,
And God was very close to them.

Sometimes, Lord, the road seems long.
I'm not always very strong.
Anyplace that I might be,
Please, dear Lord, stay close to me.
In Your name I pray. Amen.

There were no rooms left in the town,
So in a stable, crude and brown,
By piles of straw and cattle stall,
God's little Son was born for all.

King of earth and heaven too,
Earth could find no room for You.
Thank You for that Christmas Day
When You came here anyway.
In Your name I pray. Amen.

The darkness in the hills was deep
As drowsy shepherds watched their sheep.
Then in a blink, the sky burned bright.
The shepherds trembled, sick with fright.

Sometimes I am frightened too.
Help me, Lord, remember You.
Take away my silly fright.
I am Yours. I'll be all right.
In Your name I pray. Amen.

An angel said, "You need not fear.
I bring good news to people here.
In Bethlehem this very morn,
The Savior of the world is born."

Help me hear that news today.
Help me hear the angel say,
"Christ is born for you and me.
Christ is born, and we are free."
In Your name I pray. Amen.

The shepherds stood there in a daze
As hosts of angels sang out praise:
"To God be glory for this birth
And peace to all He loves on earth."

Angels sang, and I will too,
"Glory, glory, Lord, to You!"
Help me sing of Jesus' birth.
Help me work for peace on earth.
In Your name I pray. Amen.

The shepherds ran to see God's Son
And knelt before Him, every one,
Then ran some more. They had to tell:
"God's Son is born, and all is well!"

Shepherds saw and shepherds told
On that Christmas day of old.
Yes, I know the story well.
Help me, Lord, to gladly tell.
In Your name I pray. Amen.

And so our little Lord was born
Into a world all tired and worn.
He came so sin and death might end.
He came to make us each God's friend.

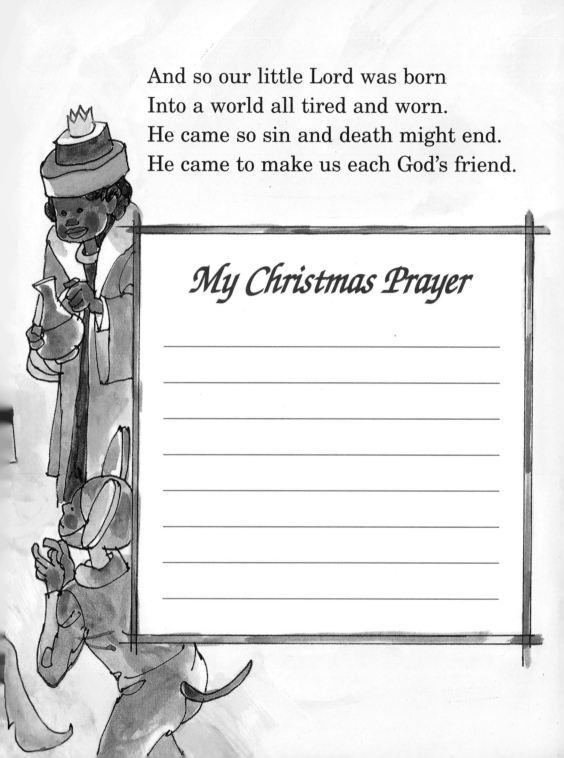

My Christmas Prayer

_____

_____

_____

_____

_____

_____

_____

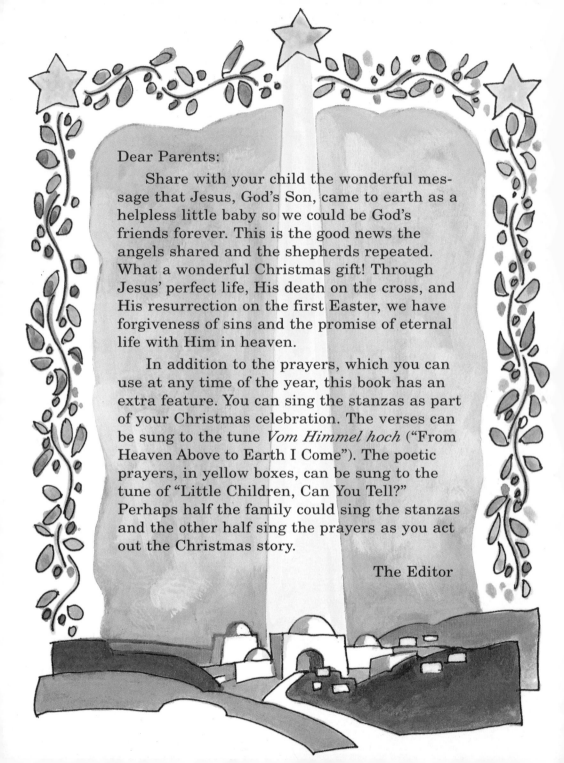

Dear Parents:

Share with your child the wonderful message that Jesus, God's Son, came to earth as a helpless little baby so we could be God's friends forever. This is the good news the angels shared and the shepherds repeated. What a wonderful Christmas gift! Through Jesus' perfect life, His death on the cross, and His resurrection on the first Easter, we have forgiveness of sins and the promise of eternal life with Him in heaven.

In addition to the prayers, which you can use at any time of the year, this book has an extra feature. You can sing the stanzas as part of your Christmas celebration. The verses can be sung to the tune *Vom Himmel hoch* ("From Heaven Above to Earth I Come"). The poetic prayers, in yellow boxes, can be sung to the tune of "Little Children, Can You Tell?" Perhaps half the family could sing the stanzas and the other half sing the prayers as you act out the Christmas story.

The Editor